SOPHIE SCHOLL
Daring Activist of WORLD WAR II

by Salima Alikhan   illustrated by Alessia Trunfio

CAPSTONE PRESS
a capstone imprint

Published by Capstone Press, an imprint of Capstone.
1710 Roe Crest Drive, North Mankato, Minnesota 56003
capstonepub.com

Library of Congress Cataloging-in-Publication Data is available
on the Library of Congress website
ISBN: 9781666333985 (hardcover)
ISBN: 9781666333992 (paperback)
ISBN: 9781666334005 (ebook PDF)

Summary: During World War II, Germany's Nazi forces stormed across
Europe, committing horrific crimes against Jewish people and others.
In 1942, 21-year-old Sophie Scholl formed a student-led, anti-Nazi
organization called the White Rose. Their goal: distribute informational
pamphlets to draw public attention to Nazi crimes—and, ultimately, stop
them. Scholl's activism and resistance eventually led to her capture and trial
before the Nazi regime.

Editorial Credits
Editor: Donald Lemke; Designer: Sarah Bennett;
Production Specialist: Katy LaVigne

Design Elements: Shutterstock/Here

All internet sites appearing in back matter were available and accurate
when this book was sent to press.

Printed and bound in the USA. 4882

TABLE OF CONTENTS

A PROMISE TO GERMANY

Sophie Scholl was born in 1921 in Forchtenberg, Germany. Her father was the mayor, and she and her five siblings had a happy childhood.

Unlike most parents, Sophie's father encouraged his kids to discuss ideas openly and think for themselves.

Papa, what does that mean?

Danger is coming. A tyrant named Hitler is trying to take over the government.

A dictator named Adolf Hitler was rising to power in Germany.

Many Germans believed Hitler's promise. He planned to build a bold new Germany. But Sophie's parents were strongly against Hitler's regime, known as the Third Reich.

We need to accept the greatness of the Third Reich! Hitler is the future! He's promising much-needed jobs!

Hitler is lying! He is a danger to us all! He wants to turn Germany into a military state!

Always think for yourself, Sophie. We must protect our freedoms and everyone's rights, even when it's hard.

But as Sophie and her siblings became teenagers, they fell under the spell of Hitler's promises. The Third Reich promised a return to nature, a love of community, and more jobs for Germans.

Sophie and her friends and siblings were excited about this vision of a bright new Germany.

Sophie joined the League of German girls, a Nazi organization. She was a talented leader and rose quickly through their ranks.

Sophie's brother Hans joined the Hitler Youth and soon received a leadership position as well.

Sophie's parents were horrified at their children's excitement about Hitler's plans.

Hitler is providing new jobs for the German people!

But look at how he is doing that! Hitler is leading Germany into another war. He wants to get rid of entire populations of people!

THE UGLY TRUTH

But soon, Nazi officials started banning all groups that were not Nazi organizations. The Nazi police, known as the Gestapo, were arresting offenders.

What's going on here?

Folk songs were no longer allowed under Hitler's regime.

It's just music! This doesn't have anything to do with Nazis!

Non-Nazi groups are now considered illegal organizations!

Hans has been arrested? For singing?

The Gestapo searched homes for evidence of illegal organizations. Anything that did not celebrate Hitler or his government was considered a threat.

When they searched the Scholls' home, they took journals, diaries, poems, and folk song collections.

I warned you about Hitler!

Hitler's control grew stronger. As the Third Reich took over, books that were considered "anti-Nazi" were burned.

Nazis also controlled what was written in the newspapers.

In Praise of the Great Hitler and the Pure Germans.

Citizens were encouraged to report anyone who opposed the Nazis. People became nervous about being watched or of saying or doing anything that might seem "anti-Nazi."

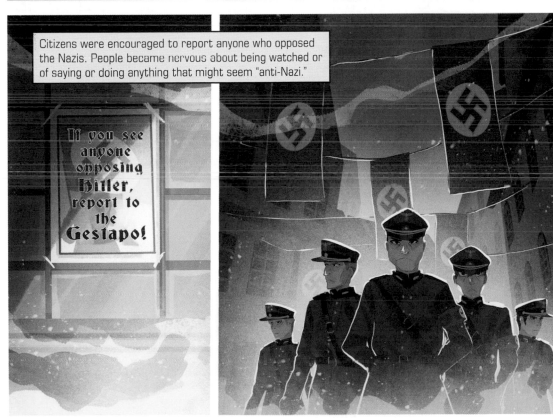

If you see anyone opposing Hitler, report to the Gestapo!

THE WAR TO END ALL WARS

On September 1, 1939, World War II began. Hitler invaded Poland. Britain and France declared war on Germany.

Sophie's brothers, Hans and Werner, were sent off to fight for Germany.

One of Hitler's biggest plans was to make others see Jewish people as less than human. He wanted to exterminate Jewish people and leave only his German "master-race."

Sophie was furious to see her Jewish friends forced to leave school.

Meanwhile, at school, students were forced to march single file, like soldiers.

Nazi officials told students that women's roles should involve "children, churches, and cakes." Sophie did not want to be told what to think

Sophie wanted to go to a university to study biology and philosophy. But before she could go, she was drafted into a six-month service to help the war effort.

I don't want to go, Mother. Hitler is not who I thought he was. I do not want to help his war.

But Sophie had no choice.

Sophie hated her assignment to help the war effort. By now she realized Hitler had lied, like her father said.

The evil of the Nazi regime made Sophie wonder about the best way to live a human life. She longed for freedom for all people.

Sophie wrote letters to her boyfriend, Fritz Hartnagel. He had been sent to fight on the Eastern Front, like her brothers had. In these letters, she poured her heart out.

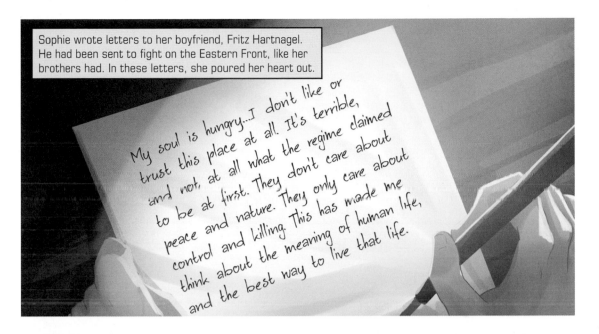

My soul is hungry...I don't like or trust this place at all. It's terrible, and not, at all what the regime claimed to be at first. They don't care about peace and nature. They only care about control and killing. This has made me think about the meaning of human life, and the best way to live that life.

Although Fritz had been drafted to fight in Hitler's war, he could see the horror of the Nazi regime. He appreciated Sophie's letters.

Once freed of her war service, Sophie was overjoyed when she arrived at last at the University of Munich. Her brother Hans was already there, studying medicine.

I'm so glad to see you, Hans! I can't wait to start taking classes!

Hans had lots to tell Sophie. He invited her to a secret meeting that night.

You can't tell anyone . . . we'll be in danger if you do!

Sophie arrived to find Hans, along with fellow students Alexander Schmorell, Willi Graf, and Christoph Probst. Like her brother, they had also served on the Eastern Front.

It's much worse than we could have imagined, Sophie. Hitler's committing horrible crimes!

Hitler is murdering Jewish people in Poland and Russia!

The boys explained to Sophie that they had already formed a secret resistance group called the White Rose. The name was supposed to represent purity and innocence in the face of evil. They had been writing and handing out anti-Nazi leaflets around town.

Sophie remembered the horrors faced by her Jewish friends back home. Her heart filled with sorrow and rage on their behalf.

Count me in. We must stop Hitler!

RESISTANCE!

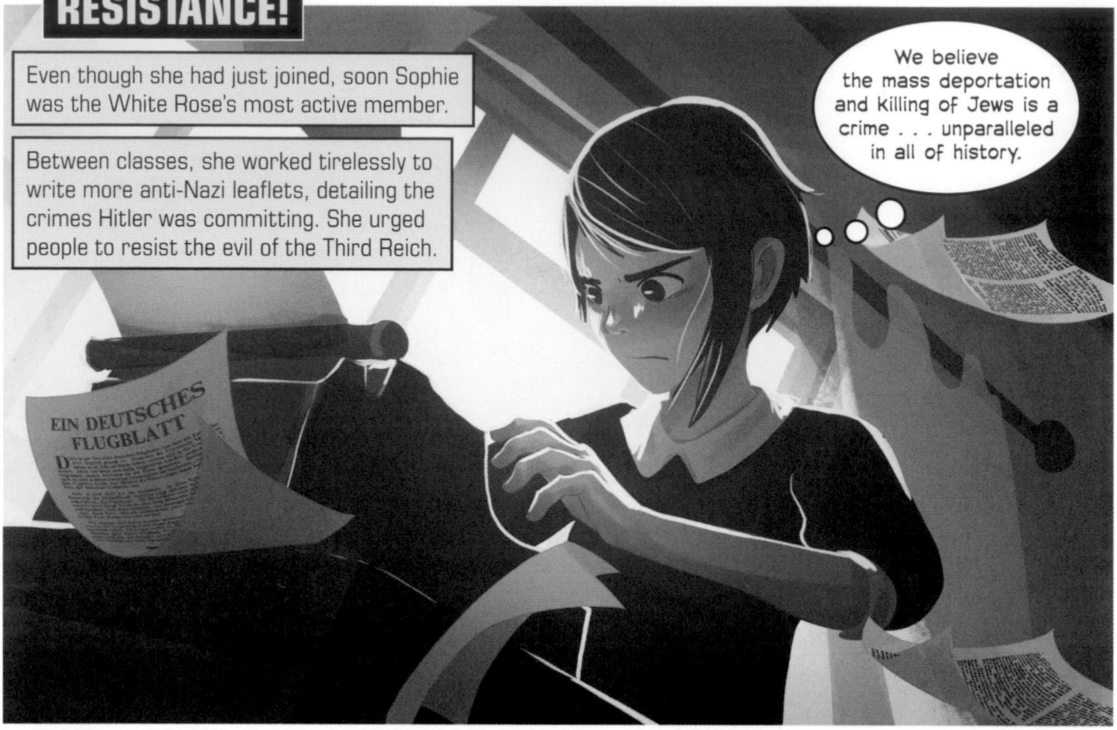
Even though she had just joined, soon Sophie was the White Rose's most active member.
Between classes, she worked tirelessly to write more anti-Nazi leaflets, detailing the crimes Hitler was committing. She urged people to resist the evil of the Third Reich.
We believe the mass deportation and killing of Jews is a crime . . . unparalleled in all of history.
EIN DEUTSCHES FLUGBLATT
unparalleled

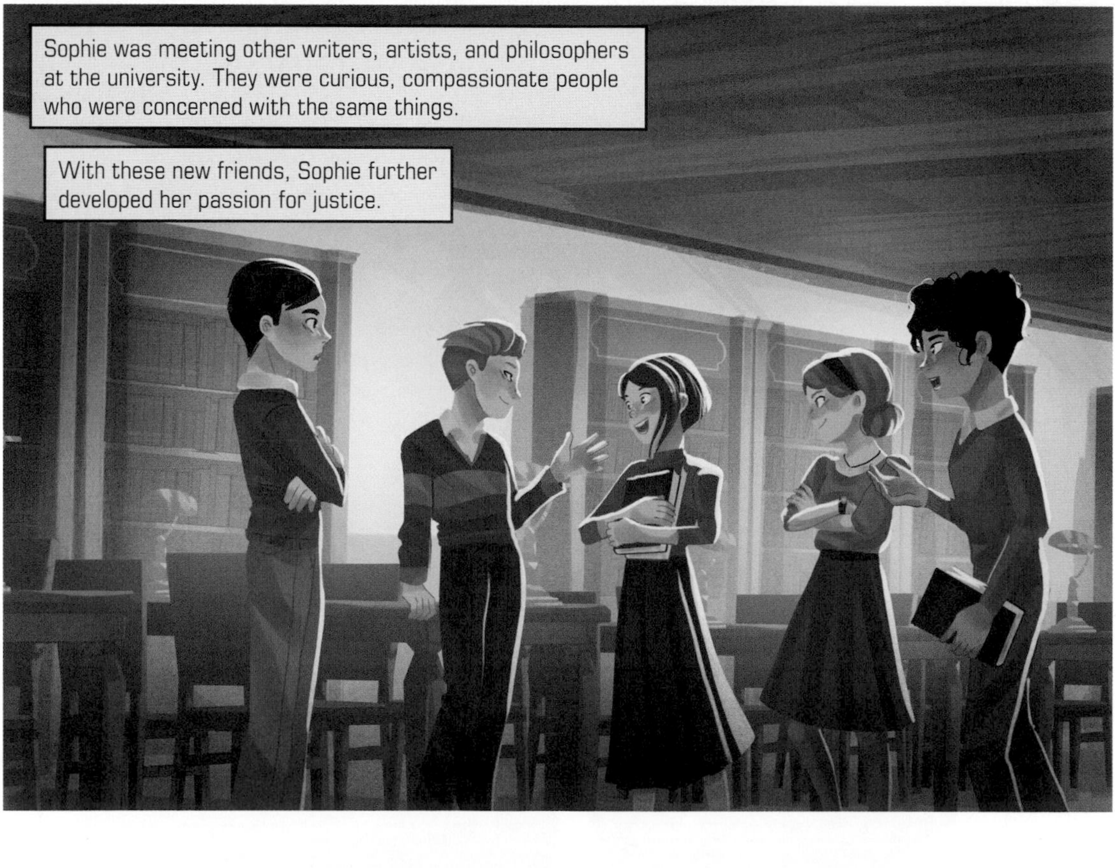
Sophie was meeting other writers, artists, and philosophers at the university. They were curious, compassionate people who were concerned with the same things.
With these new friends, Sophie further developed her passion for justice.

The White Rose mailed pamphlets in secretive envelopes so that no one would suspect what was inside. At first, their stacks of mail were small.

But soon the stacks were huge. They mailed thousands of leaflets to people all over Germany.

They spoke plainly about their beliefs, urging the German people to see past Hitler's lies.

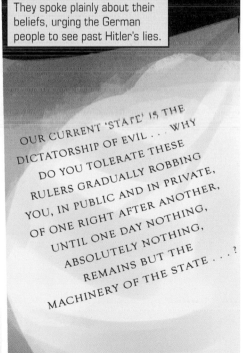

OUR CURRENT 'STATE' IS THE DICTATORSHIP OF EVIL . . . WHY DO YOU TOLERATE THESE RULERS GRADUALLY ROBBING YOU, IN PUBLIC AND IN PRIVATE, OF ONE RIGHT AFTER ANOTHER, UNTIL ONE DAY NOTHING, ABSOLUTELY NOTHING, REMAINS BUT THE MACHINERY OF THE STATE . . . ?

The White Rose worked tirelessly, day after day, writing their leaflets in secret and making copies on a mimeograph machine. They printed thousands to send all over the country.

OUR CURRENT 'STATE' IS THE DICTATORSHIP OF EVIL . . . WHY DO YOU TOLERATE THESE RULERS GRADUALLY ROBBING YOU, IN PUBLIC AND IN PRIVATE, OF ONE RIGHT AFTER ANOTHER, UNTIL ONE DAY NOTHING, ABSOLUTELY NOTHING, REMAINS BUT THE MACHINERY OF THE STATE . . . ?

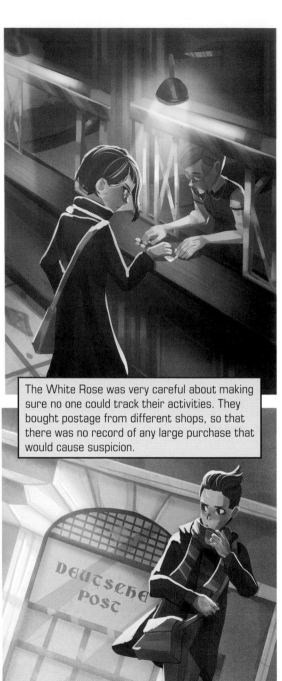

The White Rose was very careful about making sure no one could track their activities. They bought postage from different shops, so that there was no record of any large purchase that would cause suspicion.

DEUTSCHE POST

The members of the White Rose knew that their lives would be in danger if they were discovered.

They traveled to other cities to send their leaflets in secret.

They made sure that no one could track where they had come from.

On February 2, 1943, the Nazis were defeated at Stalingrad in the Soviet Union. It was the Germans' first major defeat.

The White Rose members were overjoyed at the Nazis' defeat. They hoped it meant the Third Reich was losing power.

NAZI ARMY DEFEATED AT STALINGRAD!

Emboldened, the boys of the White Rose used coal tar to graffiti anti-Hitler sentiments on various buildings in Munich.

They hoped it would spread their message to more of the public.

IT'S WORKING

People all over Germany received the White Rose's leaflets. The power of the White Rose's words reminded people of their moral duty as human beings.

Maybe they're right. Hitler is a tyrant! He hasn't helped with jobs, and the regime is only building a bigger military!

300,000 Jews have been murdered ... Hitler is guilty, guilty, GUILTY!

Many people, including students, were encouraged that others were opposing Hitler.

They're right . . . the Nazi regime isn't doing what it promised! If others are standing up against them, maybe we can too!

All over Germany, Jewish families were being imprisoned, taken to concentration camps, and murdered. The White Rose reminded people that allowing these things to happen was evil too.

This isn't right . . .

We do have a duty to oppose the Nazis. They're oppressing our freedom to think, and no society can thrive under this kind of control.

Meanwhile, Nazi officials learned of the leaflets.

Have you seen these leaflets from a group called the White Rose? They're resisting the Third Reich and causing unrest!

Where are they getting all the paper to make these leaflets? Where are they making the copies?

The Gestapo were given orders to find the people producing the leaflets.

Find them!

The Gestapo went on a rampage looking for the source of the White Rose leaflets but came up with nothing. The White Rose had done a great job making sure they were untraceable.

Do you know anything about this?

COURAGE UNDER FIRE

Unafraid, the White Rose started passing out leaflets in person, handing them to people directly.

On February 18, 1943, Sophie and Hans arrived at their university with a suitcase packed with leaflets.

Most students were in class, so Sophie and her brother rushed to distribute the leaflets in the halls before students came out of their lectures.

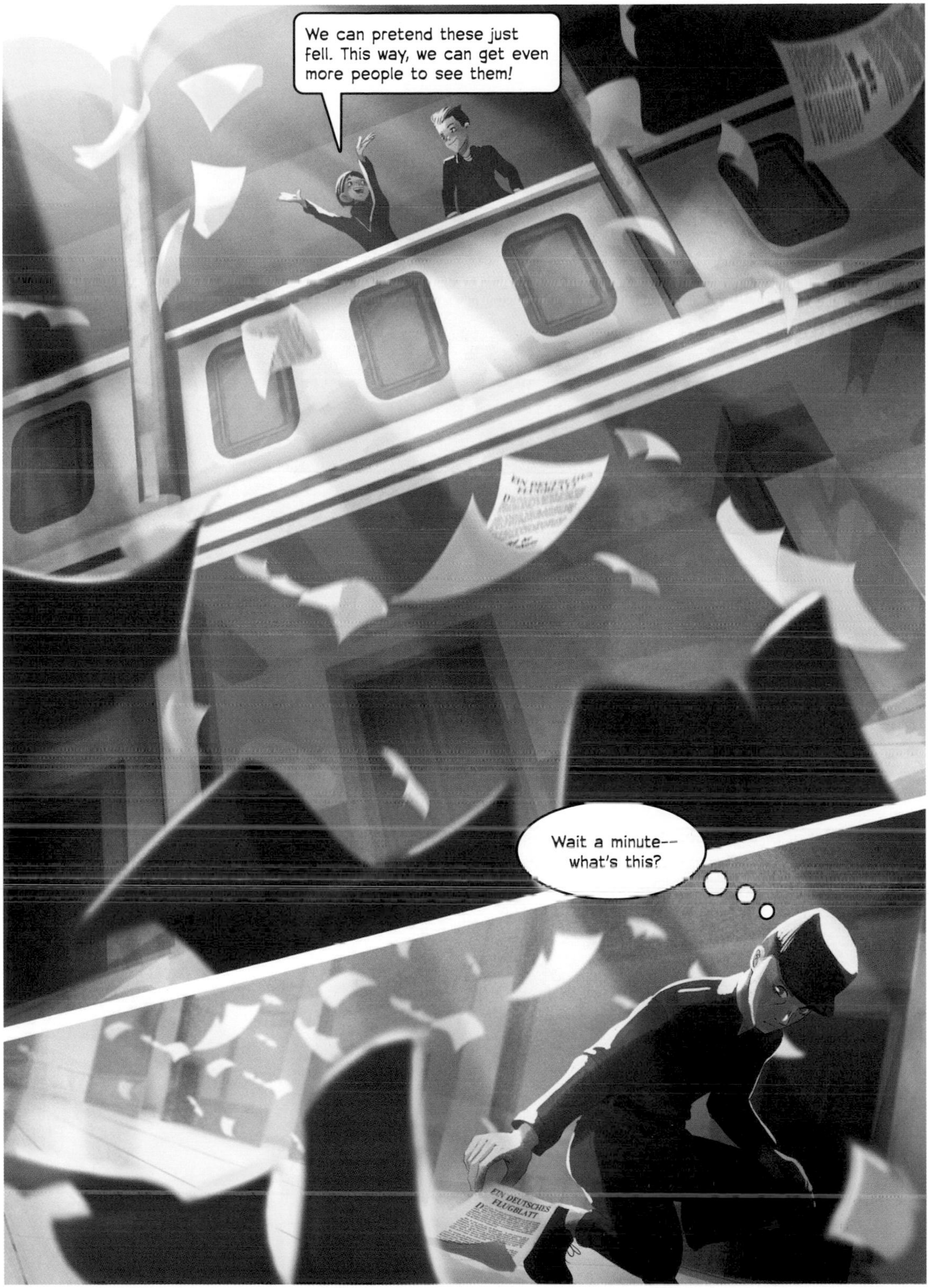
We can pretend these just fell. This way, we can get even more people to see them!
Wait a minute--what's this?
EIN DEUTSCHES FLUGBLATT

Sophie and Hans didn't know that this janitor was a member of the Nazi party.

Stop! I saw that!

These people are traitors! They're the ones who've been handing out leaflets!

Sophie and Hans were arrested. Sophie was interrogated for four days.

Miss Scholl, do you not regret your actions, and do you not feel guilty for distributing these papers and helping the Resistance?

No, on the contrary. I believe I did the best thing for my countrymen and for people everywhere. I do not regret anything, and I accept my sentence.

Even the interrogator was impressed with Sophie. He had never seen anyone so calm and brave.

If you tell the judge you were simply an ignorant accomplice of your brother's, you might get a lighter sentence.

No. My conscience told me to oppose the evil Nazi regime. I'm every bit as guilty as my brother.

Sophie and Hans were sent to trial in front of one of Hitler's favorite judges. But Sophie's voice did not shake.

Well? What do you have to say for yourself, you traitor?

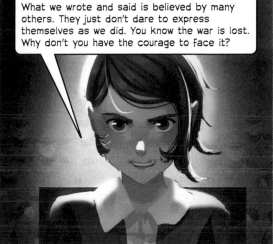

What we wrote and said is believed by many others. They just don't dare to express themselves as we did. You know the war is lost. Why don't you have the courage to face it?

Hans was also put on trial.

Hans, too, refused to be intimidated by the judge. He reminded him that once the war was over, the judge himself would be tried for war crimes.

Soon you will be standing where I now stand.

After the trial, the prison chaplain visited Sophie. He showed his support for her and for the White Rose.

There is no greater love than this—that a man should lay down his life for his friends.

LEGENDARY SOPHIE SCHOLL

Sophie, Hans, and the rest of the White Rose members were sentenced to death. But their legacy long outlived them. After the trial, one of their supporters managed to smuggle a copy of the White Rose's final leaflet into Britain.

The Allied forces loved this leaflet written by brave German students. They retitled it "Manifesto of the Students of Munich."

This is amazing! This speaks to courage and rebellion against evil!

The Allies made millions of copies of the leaflet and dropped it all over Germany.

What is this, Mother?

It's about freedom. It's saying we deserve to be free, and that we need to stand up against injustice.

Even in death, Sophie and the White Rose's message lived on.

Now, Sophie and the White Rose members are heroes and icons in Germany. They are known as students who stood up against tyranny and fought passionately for a free society.

Almost 200 schools all over Germany are named for Sophie Scholl, bearing the motto: "We stand up against injustice." She has become a legend for risking her own life to stand up for what is right.

SOPHIE SCHOLL

Sophie's courage still inspires people to make similar choices, and to stand up for others in the face of tyranny.

GLOSSARY

conscience (KAHN-shuns)—the sense that allows a person to decide between right and wrong actions

deportation (dee-pohr-TAY-shun)—the act of forcing a person to leave a country

dictator (DIK-tay-tuhr)—a person who rules with total authority and often in a cruel or brutal manner

drafted (DRAF-tid)—picked especially for required military service

exterminate (ex-TUHR-muh-nayt)—get rid of completely

gestapo (geh-STAH-poh)—a secret-police organization employing underhanded and terrorist methods against persons suspected of disloyalty

leaflet (LEEF-leht)—a usually folded printed sheet intended for free distribution

legacy (LEG-ah-see)—the mark an individual left on the world

manifesto (ma-nah-FEST-oh)—a written statement publicly declaring someone's intentions

regime (ruh-ZHEEM)—a system of rule or government

resistance (ruh-ZISS-tuhns)—a secret organization formed to oppose an army that has taken over a country

tyrant (TYE-ruhnt)—a ruler who governs absolutely with unfairness and cruelty

READ MORE

Halls, Kelly Milner. *Voices of Young Heroes: A World War II Book for Kids.* Emeryville, CA: Rockridge Press, 2020.

MacCarald, Clara. *Sophie Scholl Fights Hitler's Regime.* Lake Elmo, MN: Focus Readers, 2019.

National Geographic Kids. *Everything World War II: Facts and Photos from the Front Line to the Home Front!* New York: HarperCollins, 2021.

INTERNET SITES

BBC News: Sophie Scholl: Student Who Resisted Hitler and Inspires Germany
bbc.com/news/world-europe-57008360

Holocaust Education & Archive Research Team: Sophie Scholl
holocaustresearchproject.org/revolt/scholl.html

National WWII Museum: Sophie Scholl and the White Rose
nationalww2museum.org/war/articles/sophie-scholl-and-white-rose

ABOUT THE AUTHOR

Salima Alikhan has been a freelance writer and illustrator for 14 years. She lives in Austin, Texas, where she writes and illustrates children's books. Salima also teaches creative writing at St. Edward's University and English at Austin Community College. Her books and art can be found at www.salimaalikhan.net.

ABOUT THE ILLUSTRATOR

Alessia Trunfio is a children's book illustrator. After graduating in Animation from the International School of Comics in 2013 in Rome, she worked as a background artist for some of the most important animation studios. After a few years she decided to start a career as an illustrator. She currently works with the New York illustrator agency Astound and has published for many international publishers.